M000231556

CLEAN LOVE
IN COURTSHIP

By

REV. LAWRENCE G. LOVASIK, S.V.D.

TAN Books
Charlotte, North Carolina

Imprimi Potest   Robert Hunter, S.V.D.
                      Provincial, Girard, Pa.

Nihil Obstat ✝ Rt. Rev. A. H. Wiersbinksi, LL.D.

Imprimatur   John Mark Gannon, D.D. D.C.L., LL.D.,
                      Bishop of Erie

ISBN: 978-0-89555-095-8

Cover design by Milo Persic.

Originally published by Fathers Rumble and Carty,
Radio Replies Press, Inc., St. Paul, Minn., U.S.A.

Complete and Unabridged.

Printed and bound in the United States of America.

TAN Books
Charlotte, North Carolina
www.TANBooks.com
2013

CONTENTS

FOREWORD

My dear young friend:

This booklet contains heart-to-heart advice to safeguard your deepest and most enduring happiness. It points out to you the many dangers you will meet with along your way of company-keeping and the various aids God gives you to preserve your youthful love pure and happy. If these danger-signals are faithfully observed, you will shy away from the treacherous quicksands of sin and the slimy serpent of lust which seeks to creep into your friendship to leave its sting of death. In placing this booklet into your hands I have no intention of robbing your young love of its innocent pleasures, but rather do I wish to ensure you good clean fun and pleasures which do not backfire. Therefore, direct your company-keeping according to the sound principles of the Church that it may square with Christ's law of honor and purity. Your love and courtship will then be fair, and you will be happy before and after marriage.

I dedicate these pages to our Lady Immaculate, the gracious Patroness of Catholic Youth, that through them she may lead you to a deeper friendship with Jesus, her loving Son and your Best Friend.

Fr. Lawrence G. Lovasik, s.v.d.

Sacred Heart Mission House
Girard, Pennsylvania

CHAPTER I

Marriage Is Sacred

Marriage is a serious life-long career, ordained by God for the highest possible natural functions. God considers this contract of marriage to be so important that He made it a sacrament. Through this sacrament grace is conferred upon the contracting parties for the proper exercise of their duties towards each other and towards their children, and for the furtherance of their happiness in the family.

The primary purpose of marriage is the bringing of children into the world. Its secondary purposes are mutual help of husband and wife in the care of the family and the allaying of concupiscence or the desires of nature. Marriage makes it possible for one to cooperate with God in the creation of life. It is the privilege of a father and a mother to be instruments that God uses to bring into the world children made in His own image and likeness, children with immortal souls, children whose destiny it is to be God's children in this world and in the next.

Though marriage has its difficulties and responsibilities, it also has its tremendous God-given rewards: love and all that love means to human life; the beauty and joy of marital relationship; children, who bless and cement the union of the parents' hearts.

Since marriage is beautifully sacred, so should be the courtship that precedes it. Your courtship must

1

be pure if it is to be happy; and pure and happy, it will provide the test of character that is necessary for a blessed and a happy marriage. Only too frequently an improper courtship results in an unhappy marriage. You will trace your broken heart and wretched life to your failure to realize the difference between love and lust in courtship.

The Danger in Personal Sex Attraction

Sex attraction in God's plan begins normally with adolescence. During the formative years immediately afterwards it serves the purpose of uniting boys and girls together in wholesome social activities. It enables them to get a proper appreciation of one another, showing their mutual dependence on, and mutual power over each other. This is *general* sex attraction.

Once sufficient maturity is reached, *personal* sex attraction follows. It differs from ordinary friendship and has a God-given purpose, namely, to attract and lock the hearts of two persons together so that each craves a complete oneness with the other. This desire to blend and share their entire lives is a perfect inducement to marriage.

But this type of sex attraction can easily prove a serious danger to your chastity because of the natural urge you have of expressing your love by kissing and embracing. In the beginning there might appear to be no danger at all because you would not think of any immodest show of affection. Nevertheless, you are emotionally thrilled just to be with this particular person who attracts you in a very special way. This emotional state is heightened by caresses, and physical passion is very easily aroused. Physical passion cannot be the aim of unmarried people in expressing their love.

Never forget the weakness of human nature! Ever since Adam fell, the appetites of the senses are no longer under the perfect command of reason. In order to subject these appetites, you must exert relentless effort and call upon the grace of God.

Young women should remember that they are generally not so strongly tempted through concupiscence as are men. The young man reacts quickly to stimulation, and such reactions bring with them an urge to just a little more intimacy, which very quickly means an urge to immodesty. If these urges are not controlled, the result is sin. A young woman, however, will very likely react less quickly in a physical way, though there is always a danger that emotion will cross the line into physical passion even in her case. But an even graver danger for her is that when her love is strongly stirred by marks of affection, she will yield to her friend's urges rather than offend him or lose him. When the fires of passion are once enkindled, a natural craving for self-surrender often overpowers her. This is the danger to chastity that is inherent in personal sex attraction.

Therefore, the impulses of personal and physical attraction, namely, the attraction of body to body, should be held in check. After marriage physical attraction has its place and is the full blossoming of the human sexual instinct. Sex is only then an aid to human perfection and a means of sanctifying and

saving your soul if it conforms with the holy law
of God.

Purity Is Beautiful

Faith tells you that the use of sexual powers according to the will of God is something beautifully
sacred, but the exercise of that same power in any
way whatsoever outside of marriage is a desecra-
tion; just as the Mass itself is the most glorious
thing in the world when said by a true priest, but
is a sacrilege of the worst kind when some imposter
goes through the same ceremonies. The Christian
attitude towards the body is one of great reverence
—reverence for something our Lord wishes to be
sacred. Your body is your soul's helpmate in its
quest for God. St. Paul says, "Your bodies are
members of Christ . . . you are Christ's." For all
these reasons you cannot use your body as an instru-
ment of sin. That body is destined to rise with
Christ in glory. At Communion Jesus plants in it
anew the seed of the Resurrection. Your body is a
temple of the Holy Ghost, for God dwells in your
soul through sanctifying grace. That temple should
never be desecrated by sin.

Chastity is the moral virtue that controls the
expression of the sexual appetite. In the unmarried
it excludes all voluntary expression of the sexual
appetite for sexual pleasure. Unchastity is grievously wrong because its evil lies in the use of a faculty
outside the purpose and plan of God and nature.
The faculty of sex has been bestowed upon man
primarily for the propagation of the race. It is to

be used only in the family and not for the benefit of the individual; otherwise it is a grievous crime against nature, and abuse of a noble faculty, a violation of God's holy law.

The virtue of purity is beautiful and most pleasing to God. The angels have no need to fight impurity. Man must wage war against the sins of the flesh, and if he remains pure in the face of these temptations, he becomes greater than the angels. Love purity as a great treasure and the fairest adornment of your soul. Let the desire for complete sinlessness get into your bloodstream. It will have a beneficial influence on your whole character, giving you a sense of self-control, a confidence that will enable you to look the world straight in the eye. You will command respect of others. That is the reason why a decent young man really respects the young woman who quietly refuses to be "pawed over" and "necked"; he wants a wife who has kept pure. A decent girl breathes a sigh of relief when she finds that a young man respects her as a human being, as a friend, and as a lady. There is nothing so beautiful and so powerful as virtuous loveliness. Riches, high position, physical beauty—none of these entrances as does sinlessness. Self-control, purity, exalts the soul while preserving it from defilement. A clean heart is a happy heart. Chastity imparts a beauty and loveliness entirely distinct from mere natural perfection of feature and grace of body. In the exercise of chastity you need not be prudish or be on the lookout for evil. On the contrary, your virtue, sustained by the Sacraments and prayer, will become your protector from vice. Guarded by the innocence of your life and the prudent exercise of modesty and dignity, you can meet your friends and enjoy their companionship in a wholesome and unaffected manner.

On the other hand, *the vice of impurity is ugly*. It is a tyrant. Once you surrender to it, you will find that it will eat away your ideals of moral goodness and will make you afraid of the open. It will breed selfishness of the worst kind. It will weaken your will and make your reason a slave to mere physical instincts, when it should be their master. God hates impurity because it is an ugly vice; God loves purity because it is a beautiful virtue, a reflection of His own infinite beauty and sinlessness.

Impurity Is Forbidden

1. The Natural Law Forbids Impurity.

God has stamped this law upon our very being and it is expressed by our conscience and a feeling of shame when we are guilty. To seek indulgence in the sex appetite without regard to its purpose, namely, bringing children into the world, is a crime against nature and the lowering of ourselves to a level below that of a beast. This purpose is lawfully sought in the state appointed by God, and that is the married state. The soul and reason must rule the body and its animal appetites. The man who thinks sensual pleasures an end in themselves to be sought quite lawfully whenever desired will himself end in a corrupt heart, an enfeebled mind, and a paralyzed will, his whole character ruined. He is a slave of the devil!

2. God's Moral Law Forbids Impurity.

Chastity is a virtue, and impurity is a vice. God forbids this vice in the sixth and ninth commandments: "Thou shalt not commit adultery." "Thou shalt not covet thy neighbor's wife."

3. Christ Forbids Impurity.

"Whosoever shall look upon a woman to lust after her, has already committed adultery with her in his heart." (Matt. 5, 28.)

"If thy right eye scandalize thee (is an occasion of sin to you), pluck it out and cast it from thee. For it is expedient for thee that one of thy members should perish, rather than thy whole body be cast into hell. And if thy right hand scandalize thee, cut it off, and cast it from thee; for it is expedient for thee that one of thy members should perish, rather than that thy whole body go into hell."

"Blessed are the pure of heart, for they shall see God." (Matt. 5, 8.)

CHAPTER II

THE SIXTH AND NINTH COMMANDMENTS

Soul-death

True happiness comes from God. It fills your heart if you live according to God's plan and His commandments. Unhappiness comes from breaking those commandments by sin. Disobedience is the spirit of Lucifer: "I will not serve"; "God can't tell me what to do."

Since mortal sin is a grievous offense against the law of God, it is the greatest tragedy in the world. The emphasis is on God. You were made His child and friend in baptism. He gives you His life, the supernatural life through the sacraments, and then in a moment of selfishness you turn your back on Him. Do not try to make yourself believe that hurting those around you is the only possible evil. God does not agree with that view. When you break God's law, you hurt God—and yourself!

Sin is called *mortal* because it causes death to your soul. It is a complete turning from God. If you do not want God in your heart, He will get out. He will not force Himself on you. And if He leaves you, He takes with Him the supernatural life—which means spiritual death for you, because without God there can be no spiritual life, no happiness either. The apostle says: "The wages of sin is death." (Rom. 6, 23.) Breaking God's law by impurity in company-keeping spells death: death of the soul through the loss of sanctifying grace; death of the peace of conscience through the crushing remorse for sin; death of the delightful consciousness of the possession of unsoiled purity; death of high ideals; death of the lofty esteem and sacred reverence two people formerly had for one another. Spiritual death of mortal sin brings misery and unhappiness in this world and eternal damnation in the next.

Sin and damnation seem to be out of tune with the spirit of our time. Just because people have stopped talking about sin, do not let yourself be fooled into thinking it must not be so bad. Sin is just as nasty and just as harmful today as it ever was. Do not excuse your shortcomings on the plea that everybody is doing it. Evil may never be done even if everybody is doing it. Because it is too much trouble to behave yourself, you cannot say it is all right to misbehave. It is God, not people, who declares what is right and what is wrong; and He is right, and His Church with Him, even though the whole world may call Him wrong. The misery of the world is due to that selfishness which puts our own pleasure ahead of God's will.

It is important to remember that three things are necessary for a sin to be mortal: 1. The thing must be *very bad,* e.g., any deliberate thought, word or deed against the sixth and ninth commandments. 2. It must be done with the *full knowledge* that it is against God. You must KNOW what you are doing. 3. The wrong must have the *full consent of your will.* You must really WANT to do it. When one of these three conditions is missing, there is no mortal sin.

1. The Sixth Commandment

The sixth commandment is: "Thou shalt not commit adultery." It forbids not only adultery, but also all actions which are contrary to the orderly propagation of the human race. The faculty of sex has been bestowed upon man primarily for the propagation of the race. It is to be used only in the family and not for the benefit of the individual; otherwise it is a grievous crime against nature and a violation of God's law.

General Principle

All sexual pleasure outside marriage, alone or with others, that is directly willed or desired, intentionally procured or permitted, is a MORTAL SIN. Therefore, it is grievously sinful in the unmarried to think, say or do anything with the intention of arousing even the smallest degree of sensual pleasure.

If, however, this pleasure has arisen and (a) there was no intention of arousing it, (b) and no danger of consenting to it when aroused, it is a VENIAL SIN only if there was at least semi-deliberate consent, otherwise there is NO SIN at all.

MORTAL SIN:

1. All impure actions that are directly willed, procured or permitted. (Sexual intercourse, intimate, passionate kissing and embracing which form the natural preliminary to intercourse; unnatural acts, such as self-abuse or sexual intimacies with a person of the same sex.)

2. All other actions performed for the purpose of arousing sexual pleasure. (To kiss improperly or to read a book, to look at pictures, to attend plays or see movies in order to arouse passion.)

3. All actions which are a near danger of performing an impure action or of consenting to illicit pleasure. (Kissing, reading of a particular type of magazine which generally leads you to lose control of yourself.) In performing these actions you are practically certain to sin. If you knowingly court such a danger, you are already showing a will to sin. Ordinarily you are obliged under pain of serious sin to avoid such occasions. If the occasion cannot be avoided, then you must find some means which will strengthen you against the danger. Some things are practically always near occasions of sin; e.g., the modern burlesque show, obscene literature that portrays adultery or fornication in an attractive manner.

VENIAL SIN:

Impure actions performed without a good and sufficient reason. (Curious and imprudent looks and reading; pondering on dangerous thoughts through idle curiosity unduly prolonged; repeated kisses by lovers, even though they intend no passion; kissing from frivolous motives.)

No SIN:

Sexual actions performed with a good and sufficient reason. Your thoughts and actions are sinless when you have a good reason for them; you may ignore the sexual stimulation that may accidentally result. (Medical examination, dancing, slightly suggestive motion pictures, generally decent picture magazines, personal cleanliness.)

But sometimes sexual disturbances arising from

physical causes, such as fatigue, from some local irritation, from nervousness, are apt to be prolonged and to be a source of very severe temptation. They become mortally sinful only when you make them perfectly voluntary by deliberately promoting, approving of and enjoying them. They are not sinful at all if you do what you reasonably can to rid yourself of any temptation involved in them. This can be done by a brief, calm act of the will, "I don't want it"; by saying a little aspiration for grace of a "Hail Mary"; by trying to divert the mind to something else that is interesting or humorous; by making a brief change in external occupation.

In Regard to Others:

In regard to others, you must always remember the great law of charity by which you are bound not to induce others to sin or to help them to sin, and you must also take reasonable means to prevent their sinning when you can do so. In such things as kissing, conversation, and choice of entertainment, you cannot simply settle the matter by saying: "It doesn't bother me; therefore it's all right." For instance, in kissing, a girl should keep in mind that a boy is more responsive physically than she; but if there is some good reason for a decent manifestation of affection, she may presume that he has the proper control of himself, unless he attempts or suggests immodesty.

2. The Ninth Commandment

The ninth commandment is: "Thou shalt not covet

thy neighbor's wife." It forbids all lustful thoughts and desires.

MORTAL SIN:

To entertain a bad thought wilfully for the purpose of enjoying it or to entertain it wilfully so that it becomes a near occasion of performing an unchaste action.

VENIAL SIN:

To think about sexually-stimulating things *without* a sufficient reason.

NO SIN:

To think about sexually-stimulating things *with* a sufficient reason.

He who wishes to keep his body clean must begin by keeping his mind clean. Indulging in morbid erotic thoughts will lead to evil deeds, and may also cause mental disturbances.

Temptation Is Not a Sin

Temptation is not a sin; it is an invitation to sin. It is a fight between your duty to obey God's law and your evil desires. As soon as *you decide to give in* to your evil desires and *you want* to disobey God's commandment, the temptation is over and you have committed a sin. You must *know* what you are doing and you must *want* to break a serious commandment of God before a mortal sin can be committed. The most violent emotional desires and the most pursuing evil imaginations do not constitute sin until your will gives consent. No temptation can harm you as long as you are sincerely seeking to remain in the friendship and the love of God. By turning your will resolutely to God and prudently avoiding the occasions of sin, you can enjoy a good conscience and peace of mind even in time of temptation.

If *doubts* should come as to whether you have consented to a temptation or not, remember that if you have the habitual will and determination to resist evil thoughts and if you have prayed, you may conclude that deliberate consent was lacking. Allow no scruple or doubt to keep you from receiving Holy Communion. Abstain only when you can put your hand on the Bible and swear that you are absolutely certain you are guilty of deliberate mortal sin.

Dependent upon the nature of the temptation, your disposition, and the circumstances, all temptations against purity in thought, desire, or act, must be met decisively either by directly opposing them or directly ignoring them. *Be prepared to meet temptation:* (a) By regular confession and frequent Holy Communion; (b) By prayer; (c) By self-denial, so that when temptation comes, your will may be strong enough to want good instead of evil; (d) By turning your mind away from bad thoughts and becoming busy with other things; By avoiding whatever may lead you into temptation (the suggestive story, the smutty joke, the lewd picture, the suggestive movie or novel, bad companions, questionable places); (f) By fighting against temptations from the very first moment they come up. (g) By loving Jesus and the Blessed Virgin sincerely.

CHAPTER III

1. Passionate Kissing

Remember that a kiss is a sacred symbol, a sign of love that must not be carelessly or casually granted to chance companions and casual acquaintances. A kiss may be the occasion of physical excitement. It usually arouses passions and excites appetites that are connected with sex; when it does this and the pleasure is deliberately sought and consented to, the kiss becomes not merely a vulgar thing, but a positive sin.

MORTAL SIN:

To indulge in passionate and prolonged kissing with the intention of arousing sexual pleasure is a mortal sin by reason of the sixth and ninth commandments.

Mortal sin is involved when the kiss is a near danger of committing serious sin; for instance, when the persons concerned know from experience that even modest acts generally lead to a loss of control on the part of one or both. "Soul-kissing" might better be named "soul-killing."

VENIAL SIN:

If sensual pleasure has arisen and there was no intention of arousing it and no danger of consenting to it when aroused.

No SIN:

To experience the so-called "thrill," a feeling of

15

joy. However, such kisses can easily prove a source of danger because they prepare the way for arousing the passions.

If you are truly in love and eligible for marriage, you do not sin by manifesting your love in a modest and moderate fashion by kissing and embracing, as long as there is reasonable assurance that you and your companion will control yourselves should passion be unintentionally aroused. And yet even then you must be moderate. A brief kiss of pure affection when meeting and in parting is proper. But when your caresses, embraces, kisses are repeated and ardent even after physical passion has been considerably aroused, there is good reason to suspect that the affection you are manifesting is conjugal, that is, that it includes the physical sphere. This would be seriously wrong. Perhaps more than ninety per cent of the vilest sins of impurity have had their beginning in such kisses. Therefore, since your caresses and kisses, though well intentioned, may quickly arouse passion and flame into lust, the wiser and safer course is to abstain from all physical contact which might lead to immoderation. Ardent kisses should be held at a high premium. They should be so priceless that only a husband given at the foot of the Altar has the price with which to buy them. This price is not gold. It is integrity. There your natural expression of love will be part of the holy Sacrament of Matrimony. You may then enjoy the human element of the passion of love in innocence and with the blessing of God.

If you are not engaged, it is unwise for you to

indulge in kissing or in similar demonstrations of intimate love. Protect yourself and the young man you love by refraining from undue familiarities; they may soon become so, if not sinful now. If you are ready to grant unmaidenly privileges to a young man, you lose just that much of his respect. He will naturally conclude that you are ready to lend your lips and affection to anybody who comes along. Sensible men want the lips that have seldom been kissed. The path that leads to the ruin of women is paved with the kisses of men. The thing that no money could have hired them to do, that no arguments could have persuaded them to do, they have been kissed into doing. No girl is safe who easily permits men to kiss her.

The "good night" kiss is especially fraught with danger. Too easily it becomes prolonged and passionate and leads to improper familiarities. Thus a pleasant evening two people have had together can be quickly spoiled. Instead of feeling the joy of a good conscience, with precious memories of happy hours spent together, you will both know the pain of an accusing conscience and the loss of peace of mind. If you value your honor and virtue, you will either forego the good night kiss altogether or else you will engage in it with the reverence and respect with which you would want your own sister to be treated in this regard. Remember that God is the third party in all your company and that His eye is on you as you part.

Do not cheapen yourself by silly, light kisses. There is one answer you can make to a man's request for cheap kissing or "necking." Ask him if he would like his own sister to kiss any man who happened to call on her. Ask him what he would advise his sister to do if she were in your place. Ask him if he would like to think that the girl he is going to marry some day had kissed a hundred men who were mere casual acquaintances. Modest womanly reserve commands respect and admiration!

2. *"Petting"* or *"Necking"*

If petting or necking is done in a way that arouses sensual pleasure in one or the other, and if these pleasures are consented to, it is a *mortal sin.*

Close contact of young bodies is intended by nature to arouse passions and passionate desires. Should these desires lead to intimate liberties and impure touches, they are serious sins. Those who are engaged to be married are allowed no exemption from the law of God. They may make use of the non-passionate kiss and embrace, unless this leads to grave sin or temptation. Even if petting and necking are mild enough not to be actually an occasion of sin, they are still vulgar, common, and dangerous.

Never stoop to petting and necking, for it is unworthy of a decent girl. Such actions as holding one another's hands, sitting on one another's lap, kissing freely, caressing, fondling, embracing, and other familiarities are very dangerous. These things arouse emotions and passions that are improper and awaken thoughts, desires, and even actions that are positively indecent. Permitting yourself to be led into serious temptations frequently ends in a fall.

You cannot be too strict in these things. Break off associating with anyone who is inclined to this cheap form of lovemaking, for lust is usually behind it. If sin is the price of a boy's company, you are a lucky girl if you never see him again. He does not love you. The reason why a young man will touch a girl impurely is simply and solely because he derives a sexual pleasure from it, a pleasure that he knows is sinful. Would he permit another to do the same with his own sister? You will hear it said, "But everyone does it." No matter how many people do it, it still is wrong because God forbids all impure thoughts, desires, words, and actions. There are many souls in hell today who said, "But everybody does it." Therefore, considering the passions of men, it is wrong and sinful to indulge in petting and necking.

A girl who is free and easy in her manners, who drinks and smokes with men, and listens to and tells off-color stories; a girl who permits a man to indulge in familiarities and take liberties with her is the type of girl who commands little respect. She may be the kind of girl that men like to play with, but she is not the sort of woman they want for a wife and for the mother of their children. Experience shows that this type of girl seldom marries; and when she does, she almost invariably marries a good-for-nothing.

3. Improper Liberties

There is no love between persons of the opposite sex which does not aim at nature's design implanted by God, namely, the bringing of children into the world. Since parenthood is unlawful outside of marriage, indulgence in free love for its own sake outside marriage and apart from all intention of marriage, is unlawful and mortally sinful. The only love-making which is morally justified is that of lawful courtship, with possible marriage in view and with all the restraints of respect and modesty proper courtship and marriage imply. Worldlings try to prove to you that sinful ways are natural and that there is no wrong in obeying certain natural impulses when they call you to indulge in thoughts, desires or acts which are against the sixth and ninth commandments. Do not deceive yourself nor permit yourself to be deceived! Impurity is not sweet, though temptation and the tempter would urge that such sin is desirable. Lust lures, but in the lure lies death. If you think of man as a high-grade animal or a cultured brute, you are not going to be very backward about taking and permitting liberties on dates and in courtship. But if you regard your friend and yourself as Temples of the Holy Ghost —which you are—then you will be very careful not to desecrate those temples, though the tendencies of the lower man forever urge you to do so. If you defile His temples, God gave you His word that He will destroy you, for St. Paul says: "If any man defile the temple of God, him shall God destroy, for the temple of God is holy, which you are." (1 Cor. 3, 17.) That destruction need not be death: most often, following sinful dating and courtship, punishment takes the shape of destruction of peace and joy in marriage. The best way to forestall so horrid a disaster is to steer clear of every carelessness in the observance of Christian modesty in company-keeping.

Nature has endowed woman with a stronger instinct for modesty than man. That is the saddest moment in a girl's life when for the first time she kneels before the crucifix or image of Our Lady and feels ashamed to look into the eyes of Jesus and Mary. The stain of a sin of impurity wiped out by one fatal sweep all the previous beauty and charm of her virtue. She has not the heart to meet her mother's loving glance by looking her fondly in the eye, but casts her eyes down self-accusingly.

Woman's welfare is more directly bound up with the preservation of chastity than that of man. It ought to be her special concern to safeguard this beautiful virtue. She can exert a special power over man in this regard, and it is her sacred duty to use this power. She can sharpen man's conscience in these matters and inspire him with a sense of reverence with respect to everything that pertains to sex. It depends largely on her whether the sex relation will be ennobled or degraded. Man is inclined to look up to her as an ideal; it is her fault if she steps down from the pedestal and cheapens herself. The fact is that woman suffers more severely from laxity in sex matters than man and that, consequently, in self-defense she must demand an absolute respect for the virtue of chastity and allow no compromise. A young woman who prevails on her fiance to approach the sacraments with her at regular intervals builds up a strong bulwark against improper advances and obtains the best guarantee for a happy future.

Nature also gave man the instinct for the maintenance of manly honor and chivalry, which prompts him to earn the respect, attachment, and love of a pure woman. Nature inclines him to be a chivalrous protector of her virtue and honor, making him willing to suffer any hardship in order to keep her innocence from every harm, as he would in the case of his own sister. When, instead of protecting a woman's virtue against others, man himself turns traitor and, to satisfy his low carnal desires, does what he can to wreck it, he disgraces his manhood, plays false to his title of Christian, and renders himself an object of scorn and disgust to the woman he seduces. A man who takes undue personal liberties with a girl is her deadliest enemy—a robber who has deprived her, not of all her money and jewels, but of her greatest possession, her spotless innocence. The meanest criminal, even if he murdered her in cold blood, would not be able to harm her as she has been harmed by her so-called "friend." A girl's worst enemy is this sort of "friend," who, demon-like, desecrated and devastated the beautiful temple of her soul.

The preservation of chastity depends on the presence of honest and genuine love. He who sincerely loves will keep the proper distance and will not allow the bloom to be worn off the flower of love by cheapening, immoral intimacies. True love gives strength of character and assists in the acquisition of self-control. It never takes advantage of another for the sake of personal gratification.

To preserve bodily integrity before marriage, a young man must also possess some knowledge of women. Good and pure-minded women inspire respect and make the task of a young man easy, for he will have no difficulty in keeping the right distance. A self-respecting young man will have nothing to do with girls of loose morals who hold themselves cheap and sell their favors like wares. But it is the height of chivalry to deal with an intermediary group: thoughtless, superficial girls, who play with fire. They test to the utmost the character of a good young man. He must protect these silly creatures against their folly and against his own passions which they foolishly arouse.

In order that a *young man* may keep the virtue of chastity intact in himself and in his prospective lifemate, he must firmly believe in the possibility of a chaste life before marriage and be convinced that God demands sexual abstinence outside the married state. God imposes no duty that is beyond our power, and He knows well what man can accomplish aided by His grace. This realization will influence the young man's attitude towards his fiancee and make him feel ashamed of any improper intimacies.

Very wisely a decent girl will conclude that if her lover insists on indulging in mutual indecent liberties in courtship, and if he cannot master himself in the period immediately preparatory to marriage, when this mastery is comparatively easy, she cannot expect him to control himself after marriage, when control is likely to be more difficult. What chance would she have for salvation and happiness in a marriage in which her partner would be a constant occasion of sin to her?

The loss of chastity will be a terrible memory in afterlife and a source of painful reproach. Chastity untarnished will be a source of moral strength and the best guarantee of fidelity in the marital union.

A frequent reason for cursed marriages is the folly of couples who under the screen of courtship usurp the privileges of married life without assuming the burdens of it. Had they abstained from illicit love-making in their courtship, God would have blessed them with the sacred and lasting love the Sacrament of Matrimony and its subsequent blessings bestow. Since they loved in an unholy way before they married, God consigns them to a loveless life after their marriage. Not infrequently they must bemoan in vain their punishment or trial of not having children. Nature has its fixed purposes and limits. Once these are wilfully perverted, ignored or ruthlessly exhausted by immoral practices, no regret or promise of betterment will ever restore nature's forces to their productive power. Against such sins St. Paul warns, "Be not deceived: God is not mocked. For what things a man shall sow, those also shall he reap. For he that sows in his flesh, of the flesh also shall reap corruption. But he that sows in the spirit, of the spirit shall reap life everlasting." (Gal. vi. 7, 8.)

When you prepare for a date, you may make yourself as attractive as possible; that is the sensible thing to do if you do it with a good intention, that is, to show that you respect both your escort and yourself by making yourself as innocently inviting as you can, but by all means be reserved and hold your treasures from rough hands and evil desires. Rather die than permit yourself to be embraced and kissed by the men who seek your company and extend their social courtesies only to demand that you pay by surrender to their desires. The man takes you to the movie, to dinner, to a dance, to a party, or for an automobile drive, but you owe him no liberties for this. If you are an earnest Catholic girl, you will retain the grace of God and your self-respect, while enjoying the esteem of all good men. You will even make evil minds pause, dazzled by the purity in your eyes, the modesty of your actions, and the reserve in your words.

4. The Parked Car

Enemy number one to the chastity of young people is the parked car. With the cloak of darkness and seclusion thrown around them, young couples parked along country roads are deliberately subjecting their virtue to a great and violent strain. Parked automobiles, scenes of passionate kissing, petting and necking, are truly graveyards in which are buried the innocence and purity of thousands upon thousands of young men and young women. Here so-called love turns out to be lust, the most selfish sin, which seeks impure self-satisfaction at the expense of another's virtue.

If you are a decent girl, do not drag down a young man into the mire of impurity by consenting to have him park his car, thus giving him a favorable occasion for sin. Even under favorable conditions every young man has to struggle to keep pure. God said, "He who loves the danger will perish in it." Therefore avoid the parked automobile as you would a pest house, reeking with germs of fatal maladies.

At the end of the evening's entertainment, do not let your friend accompany you into your home, but bid good night when you arrive there. This will be a protection for you both. To do otherwise at that time of night, when the other members of the family have retired, is to subject each other to substantially the same danger as that presented by the parked car. Many a pure courtship has been ruined through the failure to heed this caution.

5. Drinking

It is not a sin to drink, but it is always a sin to drink too much. If through excessive drinking you lose the use of reason, you commit a *mortal sin* and thereby descend to a level lower than that of the brute beast.

Even if drinking does not end in drunkenness, its effects on company-keeping are disastrous. Drink adds fuel to concupiscence and increases the force of temptation to impurity; it weakens the powers of the mind and lowers the resistance of the will, thereby leaving one open to sin. Drink has always been one of the shortest roads to moral corruption and is the greatest contributing factor to the alarming increase of crime. Facts show that liquor figures in seven out of every ten crimes. Drinking outside the home is usually the beginning of the drinking habit and other bad habits, especially impurity. Many a young man and young woman who normally would not think of lust have ruined their courtship and destroyed their love through drinking.

Do not fall a prey to this habit just to be sociable. To say that a party without drink lacks good-fellowship and sociability is stupid and betrays a low mental status. Among young and intelligent people drink should be in no sense necessary for a good time. If you really prize your virtue and demand self-respect, do not drink at all. The achievement of true and clean happiness is worth the little act of self-denial involved in abstinence from alcoholic drink. The fact that about three-fourths of broken homes are the consequence of drinking should be an argument strong enough to make you give up associating with anyone who, having a special liking for alcoholic drink, does not know how to control himself.

6. Indecent Entertainment

Another danger in company-keeping arises from frequenting burlesque theaters, night clubs, road houses, and taverns where salacious floor shows, off-color jokes, and expensive drinks are the chief menu. In these places semi-nude females perform lascivious dances and fill young minds with obscene jokes, plying them with drinks and turning them into sex-crazed maniacs. These are the agencies which poison innocent minds and prevent their normal development into wholesome manhood and womanhood, sending them out as criminals to prey upon society.

In our day perhaps the deadliest misinformant about the ways of true living is the motion picture show. Sometimes the scenes are so vivid that for all practical purposes young people might just as well be acting in the presence of men and women who are disregarding God's holy laws. Such indecent attractions offered by the screen lower ideals and distort the standards of young Catholic men and women. It has become all too common for those born and reared in the faith to forget the lessons they have learned: that their thoughts, desires, and acts must be chaste; that all near occasions to sin must be avoided; that the most priceless thing in the soul of a girl is her purity, and the noblest virtue in the young man is preservation of his moral integrity. Many a boy and girl can testify that he or she was guilty of the first grave lapse from chastity after having witnessed scenes of love-making and lustful seduction created by much publicized movie stars. Start a fire, inhale the flames of lust, and your soul will die. Let the Legion of Decency be your guide in regard to the choice of pictures. Refrain from seeking pictures that are even partly objectionable.

7. Immodest Conversation
Speaking

MORTAL SIN:

Immodest conversation with the intention of exciting the hearers to lust. Course language which would scandalize and excite the young and innocent.

VENIAL SIN:

Immodest conversation which is merely suggestive or slightly objectionable.

NO SIN:

Serious conversation about sexual topics is permissible when there is a sufficient reason for it and proper precautions are taken.

Listening

MORTAL SIN:

To listen to obscene conversation for the sake of the sensual pleasure that it excites.

VENIAL SIN:

To listen out of curiosity or to laugh at obscene jokes from human respect.

Many people who tell stories with sexy content are not bothered by them, but they have to assume some responsibility for their listeners. Things like this can easily give scandal, especially in a mature mixed group, and above all when adolescents are present. The mere fun of telling a story is never a sufficient reason for the uncertain danger of temptation which is practically always present.

A smutty story displays your lack of a sense of decency and the state of your soul. It proclaims the meagerness of your sources of entertainment, the coarseness of your ideas of humor, the inadequacy of your means of expression. It soils the imagination of your hearers, hanging vulgar pictures in the inner chambers of their minds. A dirty story disgusts people of finer sensibilities who care for the clean, wholesome things of life, but hate dirt. It dishonors your parents, your friends, your God and yourself!

Off-color and suggestive stories and jokes may be serious occasions of sin in company-keeping. They easily arouse passions and lead the way to sin. Make it a point of honor that you will never soil your date with a single dirty story. Say nothing that you would not want your mother to hear. God sees and hears you. Never take wilful pleasure listening to a dirty story. If you are not in a position to silence the story-teller or change the trend of conversation, or leave, at least refrain from encouraging him by your interest or expression of pleasure and approval. Let him see from your attitude that you are not interested. Avoid the company of those who tell filthy jokes or stories. If your friend belongs to this class, you have made a very poor choice.

8. Dangerous Reading

MORTAL SIN:

The reading of a very obscene book without sufficient reason. The reading of slightly objectionable books with an evil intention.

VENIAL SIN:

The reading of slightly objectionable books out of mere curiosity and without evil intentions, e.g., a novel with too passionate love.

NO SIN:

Those who have a serious reason for reading (doctors, nurses, spiritual directors, teachers, young people about to be married who need instruction) do not sin, even though they should be strongly excited, provided that they control their wills. The greater the danger to the virtue of chastity, the greater must be the justifying reason for reading dangerous books. Even mere entertainment justifies one in ignoring occasional slight motions of passion caused by a few suggestive pictures or passages in books or magazines that are otherwise decent. But mere entertainment is not usually a complete justification for reading things that one finds strongly stimulating, even in an otherwise decent book or magazine.

One of the great enemies to the moral cleanliness of youth is the avalanche of filth being poured upon them today by smutty magazines, lewd pictures and newspapers which relate the details of sexual crimes and divorce scandals. Such literature poisons the minds, befouls the imaginations and sullies the hearts of youth. The publishers of these filthy, sex-inciting magazines are the arch criminals of our day, the criminals who turn out others by the hundreds.

Make it a point of honor never to read any literature which you know to be in any way objectionable. Refrain from reading cheap books and magazines that will scarcely be an inspiration to you. Read and promote Catholic books, magazines and pamphlets in order to become a better Catholic and help the cause of truth and virtue. You cannot appreciate anything you know little about.

CHAPTER IV

PRACTICAL TIPS ON DATING

Three General Principles

1. Always Keep Your Courtship on a High Plane

Keep sex in the background! It must not dominate your thoughts and dictate your conduct. The physical must be subordinated to the spiritual because man is a spiritual creature and not mere animal. Allowing your courtship to degenerate to the physical would mean a loss of honor and respect. An attraction which springs largely from the physical element of sex is an insecure foundation for enduring friendship and conjugal love.

Pure love is the foundation of a happy courtship. The reason why there are so many sinful, saddened hearts in courtship is because too many young men and women fail to distinguish clearly between love and lust; and yet they are as completely different as day is from night. True love is pure, beautiful, noble, self-sacrificing. It is dominated by mutual respect for each other's character, not by mere emotion, passion and lust. True love is unselfish, thinking only of the good of the other; it would rather endure any self-restraint than harm the other in any way. If love-making does not rise above the mere thrill of bodily sensations, it can be no more than indulgence in passion, which is lust.

Lust, on the other hand, is ugly, base, selfish, impure; it seeks nothing outside itself. All fine promises and sweet expressions of love are but lies. A

32

beautiful friendship is marred because the boy and girl permit indecent liberties which are like vicious cancers eating their way into their very hearts and destroying virtue, peace and happiness. Pure love is the best preparation for marriage; lust draws down God's curse upon it. If by company-keeping you are encouraged in purity, the true love is the basis of your friendship and enduring affection will be the result. If through company-keeping you are encouraged to impurity, then lust, not love, is the foundation of the friendship and evil will be the result. There is a natural and necessary relationship between your conduct now and your status later in marriage. If a young man is selfish, loose, crude, unreasonable now, do not expect that he will be unselfish, high-minded, spiritual and controlled in marriage. The Sacraments do not change nature; they elevate it if it is disposed to be elevated.

A foul love must be driven out by a fair love. In the pure love of a young man for a virtuous girl, he finds a shield against unchastity. Reverent love will be a protection for both. If a boy wants the girl he goes with now to be the best wife she can be for his children; if he himself wants to be the best husband he can be for her and the best father he can be for his children, he must respect that girl before marriage. He will do everything he can, in a positive way, and at any price, to retain or regain his personal purity and to protect the modesty and loveliness of the girl he respects, even as St. Joseph kept himself spotless and safeguarded the virginity of the Mother of God.

Consequently, you need not resort to lust to enjoy one another. You will find untold happiness in the mere presence of the one you really care for—happiness which arises from the contact of mind with mind, of heart with heart, of personality with personality. This is infinitely more satisfying and enduring than mere contact of bodies. Wondrous beauty can be found in the character of any good boy or girl if you will only patiently look for it. A young man will surely win the heart of a girl if he always acts as a gentleman and places her upon her rightful pedestal of innocence and queenly modesty. In like manner, a girl will command the respect and win the love of a boy if by words and actions she makes it clear that she will tolerate no compromise with her ideals of honor and integrity. Any momentary weakness may be implied as an invitation to dangerous liberties.

Direct your friendship so that it may square with Christ's law of honor and purity in a chaste and noble love. Elevate your love to Christ that your love may be sweeter and more enduring. Then leaving one another, you can walk to the Communion rail and receive your Eucharistic Lord with reverent minds and chaste hearts. Where chaste love fills your company-keeping, courtship becomes an aid to virtue and an encouragement to holiness.

2. Follow a "Hands-off" Policy

The purpose of courtship is to prepare you for marriage by enabling you to find the boy who will one day be your partner in life; hence it is to be spent in the manner God has intended. Anything that is contrary to God's holy law in courtship should be avoided, lest the devil, and not God, rule your friendship and lead it most certainly to moral disaster.

Too many perfectly decent and innocent girls do not understand a young man's problem of self-control. Many dangers and temptations will be avoided if you remember that the physical element of sex is more highly localized in man and that he is more easily aroused, while the psychical element is more pronounced in woman. Actions and contact which leaves you undisturbed may greatly arouse the passions of your companion. Consequently, be considerate of him as well as of yourself and discourage any liberty which may be an occasion of sin. An earnest word, a look of disapproval, a sudden change in the conversation, a quick and determined step away will be a hint that a decent young man will not fail to take. With his senses restored to him, he will appreciate this firm yet sympathetic gesture and will admire you all the more for it because he will see that you really want to keep your courtship clean. On the other hand, if you yield to his entreaties for certain liberties, he will be ashamed of himself for his humiliating defeat and disgusted with you (though he may not show it) because you occasioned it. You will equally share in this feeling of shame and disgust, especially if you realize that your womanly modesty should be your greatest treasure.

It is therefore wise and even necessary for you to follow a "hands-off" policy. Respect the person of the friend with whom you are keeping company and make him respect you. Do not try to set him —and yourself as well—on fire by exciting desires which cannot be satisfied save at the expense of all that you both should hold dear. Love should occasion happiness, not pain; so do not torture your friend by inflicting on him restlessness and a disturbed conscience. To refrain from the defilement of the good and to allay lust in the hearts of men is the greatest human victory that woman can win over man. She then becomes close to the angel in appeal.

3. Plan Your Dates

If you have to plan for the prolonged date that is marriage, you are smart if you plan for even the brief date of a day or an evening together. A marriage without interests or things to do is dull and dangerous. To go off on an unplanned date with nothing in particular to do is also dull and often dangerous. At the end of the date the boy finds that he has spent a lot of money on a lot of things that did not give either of you a great deal of fun. The girl finds that she is expected to accept or is forced to resist a vigorous effort on his part to fill out a flat, unplanned date with adolescent love-making.

Dates are successful when they are planned. That means that you ought to look around for unusual and interesting things to do, novel places to visit, pleasant things to talk about. But a date is not merely a recreation quest—dancing, the theater, the movies, going places. A date really is anything that two or more people enjoy doing together. Real fun is found not on dates where a lot of things are done for you, but on dates where you are doing things yourself.

Dates lose their charm if you assume that they must be expensive. You can have more fun walking with someone you like than you can dining at a fashionable restaurant, paying a heavy cover charge and checking an expensive menu merely to impress somebody who may not even want to be impressed. A bank-roll is not the essential factor of a good time. A girl who has to have a lot of money spent on her before she has a good time on a date will make a nagging, money-digging, selfish sort of wife. A boy who will not ask a girl out unless he has a pocketful of money is a show-off. Worth-while girls do not expect a man to spend a lot of money on them. Be honest about the fact that you have not a lot of money to spend. Your city is full of places to go and things to do that do not cost much more than a little walk or carfare. You can spend very happy hours wandering with a pleasant companion through a park, an art gallery, a museum, an industrial center, a beautiful church, or listening to a good lecture or a band concert. Hobbies can enter into the schedule of dates—things you do extremely well, things you are interested in collecting. A girl should be interested in what interests the boy she likes. A boy probably gets more zest out of his hobby if he thinks that some pleasant girl is interested in it, too.

It is often advisable to add another couple to your dates if you find each other a temptation and danger; this is better than giving up dating altogether. This self-chaperoning often eliminates a lot of problems for both the boy and the girl. Be interested in four-some or sixsome dates. Talking is simpler and there is more fun. It ceases to be a dialogue, or, worse, a monologue. Double dating need not be expensive if expenses are shared. Temptation is much less likely when there is a small crowd. Then, too, a foursome or a sixsome on a date can take part in games, which are often very exciting. All this means more dates at home; more dates where money does not have to be considered; where the radio brings the music of the greatest name orchestras in the nation right into your living room; where a record-ing machine and a supply of records keep a crowd going for an evening; where a homemade sandwich tastes delicious; where the piano becomes the center of fun, and a crowd put their heads together to sing to their own delight. Thus dates could be built around that very normal love that both boys and girls have for good youthful talk. This sort of date will cut the occasion for adolescent love-making to a minimum.

Your dates will be happy if they are sinless. The people you go out with should be better because they were with you. Do not permit yourself to be touched by any of the things that make so much modern dating ugly and perilous—too much drink, dirty stories, disgusting dances, questionable taverns and roadhouses, sin and all its ugliness. Foresee and guard against the dangers that might spoil your dates.

Always take Jesus and Mary along with you on

your dates. They are deeply happy to see you happy. There is something terrible in the thought that, while sorrow often drives young people to the feet of Christ and Our Lady, good times are often occasions for driving Jesus and Mary from their side, when they hold out their arms to evil. When you are going out on a date, why don't the two of you make a call on Christ in the tabernacle? You should make a date to go to benediction, to the novena, to May devotions, to confession, to a special sermon, as naturally as you go to a movie or dance. Make a date to go to Mass and Holy Communion together before you start off on your hike, your picnic, your day in the country. You can do nothing better than to make dates that include Jesus and Mary. There is no better company! Nothing could make your date happier.

"Don'ts" on Dates

Though the following suggestions are directed mainly to girls, they are equally applicable to boys, inasmuch as boys will know what is expected of a decent girl and will cooperate with her in preserving her virtue.

1. Don't forget that the *chastity* of your soul and your good name are your most precious possessions; protect them by mutual self-respect. Therefore, always keep your courtship on a high plane and follow a "hands-off" policy and by your manner give men to understand that your loveliness is not to be marred by unruly passion and sin.

2. Don't permit expressions of love or friendship for another to be prolonged to the point of *danger*

of lust because all sexual pleasure outside marriage, that is directly willed, intentionally procured or accepted is a mortal sin. A selfish indulgence of your own passions regardless of the welfare of the one you "pretend" to love is not really love, but lust.

3. Don't ever permit *passionate kissing* to mar your date, for true love is dominated by mutual respect for each other's character, not by mere emotion, passion and lust.

4. Don't be so soft as to pay for an evening's entertainment with *cheap kisses, "necking"* and *"petting,"* because a man who is not strong in chastity will probably take all you will give. A decent man, even though he may be weak, does not respect that kind of girl. Don't give a casual friend the caresses that belong only to the good Catholic man you will some day meet, who will be your husband and the father of your children.

5. Don't be so *imprudent and reckless as to date this one and that one without knowing anything about them beforehand.* Avoid being alone with strangers.

6. Don't consent to keep company in a *parked car,* for darkness and seclusion are favorable conditions for sin.

7. Don't allow your escort *to enter your home late at night* after a date; this would subject you both to danger and suspicion.

8. Don't fall into the bad habit of permitting long *"goodnights"* and *"passionate goodnight kisses."* These have brought about the death of many a friendship and killed many a soul.

9. Don't encourage a young man to *visit your home too frequently,* or to protract his visits far into the night or early morning, to the discomfiture of your family and the detriment of your own and your fiance's health, virtue, and reputation. Turning night into day three or four times a week in courtship is not a good recipe for the preservation of health or the increase of corporal fitness; this is particularly true if the long visits are accompanied with an emotional strain.

10. Don't seek out or continue companionship with others whom you know to be inclined to *evil jests and words.* Never let your date be marred by a single filthy story, but show your displeasure at once.

11. Don't take part in *dances* that may be a source of temptation to yourself or others. In dancing, don't hold your partner too tightly, lest you become an occasion or a cause of sin.

12. Don't go to see *movies* rejected by the Legion of Decency; even those that are partly objectionable should be avoided.

13. Don't frequent *taverns or roadhouses* of questionable character; this is a disgrace to womanhood.

14. Don't drink *intoxicating liquor;* it prepares the way for immorality by arousing the passions, blurring the mind, and weakening the will.

15. Don't *dress unwisely* so as to invite lustful interest, but becomingly, so as to accentuate your best gifts.

16. Don't *smoke,* not because it is morally wrong,

but because it cheapens your personality and detracts from your womanly charm.

17. Don't hold to the opinion that the only enjoyable date is *an expensive date*. Real fun is found not on dates where a lot of things are done for you, but on dates where you are doing things together. Get interested in foursome or sixsome dates; they cut the need for adolescent lovemaking to a minimum.

18. Don't fail to *avoid dangerous occupations* in courtship, or permit yourselves to be too much alone. Rather, take part in healthy worth-while hobbies and pastimes which you find mutually delightful and in which you can indulge without loss of mutual esteem or virtue. Enjoy good music; read and discuss worth-while literature; attend respectable dances and social pastimes, preferably such as are given under Catholic auspices and with proper supervision; frequent unobjectionable shows on the stage or on the screen; go on hikes with other young people and take an active interest in various wholesome sports.

19. Don't be so snobbish as to think that the *social activities of your parish church* are not good enough for you. You should feel privileged and honored to contribute to others' success by your presence and cooperation.

20. Don't get involved in a friendship that may result in a *mixed marriage*, for married life is difficult enough without having a difference of religion and moral outlook as a cause for further trouble, such as the question of divorce, birth control, Catholic education.

21. Don't disregard the *voice of your conscience* upon returning from a date. If that voice is joyous and peaceful, your company-keeping is good and clean. If it is sad, remorseful, accusing, something is wrong in your company-keeping, something that must be corrected at once or else the company-keeping must cease. The state of your conscience is a decisive test.

22. Don't get serious about *a boy who is not willing to prove himself* by avoiding sin, especially impurity and drunkenness, frequenting the sacraments at least each month, and spending a reasonable amount of time in prayer daily. Never think of marrying someone who will not be able to make you better for living with him, for the foundation of a happy marriage is a holy love which will enable you to aid each other to practice virtue and fulfill your duties.

23. Don't neglect to *use the means of grace* God has given you to keep pure. The best protection against falling a prey to one's passions is regular Confession and frequent Holy Communion (preferably each week, or even daily), because these sacraments give you special actual graces to help you practice virtue and avoid sin. Other aids are daily Holy Mass, the cultivation of will power through little acts of self-denial, the avoidance of dangerous occasions of sin, the counsel of one's regular confessor, the reading of good books, the companionship of virtuous friends, the daily Rosary and frequent recourse to God and Our Lady in prayer.

Teen-age Dating

Dear Teen-ager:

Company-keeping prepares you for marriage. Every date has an influence upon your future. You sometimes need forcible reminders lest wild desire for fun bring tragedy. Right or wrong companions can make or break your life. You should know exactly what is morally right and wrong on dates; this you will learn from the contents of this booklet. Though girls or boys don't rush madly out to sins of impurity, all too often they are tricked into what they were not properly warned against. Now God gave you a fourth commandment: "Thou shalt honor thy father and thy mother." Your conscience tells you to obey your parents as God's representatives. They are responsible for you. They are right in fearing moral dangers from "solo" dates and friendships with doubtful characters. They also have a right and duty to make rules regulating your dates, because they really want to protect your fun and your future. The best thing to do is sit down with your mother or father and talk things over. They are your best friends. Let them decide what is right or wrong. Obey the rules they make concerning your life, and dating in particular.

Keep in Mind the Following Simple Suggestions

1. You must have permission for dates. Permission can be given on a general basis (every Friday night you may attend school games and parties); or on a date-by-date basis (you may go to the basketball dance next Saturday). Your mother and father need not know each detail of dates, but they

should have the general picture.

2. Always ask permission if you intend to be away all night; this should be only with families your parents know and trust.

3. Your parents have a right and duty to make some rules about cars and about the beginning and end of dates. The boy should call for the girl at her home, come in and meet the folks, bring her home and say good-bye (not at great length) at the door. Prolonged farewells in cars easily become danger-ous. It is sometimes best to keep your dates on a group basis, that is, house parties, dances, skating parties. Group dates can be frequent in high school; "solo" dates should be spaced out. Too much dating can very soon breed violent infatuation. And fa-miliarity breeds a lot more than contempt; it leads you into sin. Silly "going steady" (exclusively with one boy or girl) has ruined many a promising youngster and even many a possible good marriage.

4. Build up ideals in your mind. Obey rules be-cause you are convinced they are sensible; this is far better than blind or reluctant obedience. Obey and respect your parents because they have your wel-fare at heart and wish to please God and protect your future.

5. Your best assurance of a pure and happy youth is a close and tender friendship with Jesus and Mary. Such a friendship is fostered by at least monthly Confession, frequent Holy Communion (weekly, or even daily), regular prayer, especially the daily Rosary.

CHAPTER V

AIDS TO CHASTE COMPANY-KEEPING

Your most powerful ally in your noble struggle for decency is your religion. It takes you by the hand, guiding you over the pitfalls that beset your way, and puts your feet safely upon the paths that lead to the sunlit mountain peaks of nobility of character and purity. Not only does it make clear the moral law and supply sanctions for its observance, but it offers you aids to carry out that law.

While the preservation of purity calls for a constant and determined struggle, you are not struggling single-handedly. God is always ready and willing to help you with His grace. "God is faithful, who will not suffer you to be tempted above that which you are able, but will make also with temptation issue, that you may be able to bear it." (Cor. 10:13.) With God's all-powerful help, you can win every victory. This grace of God is obtained through the sacraments, prayer, self-denial, and a tender love for Jesus and Mary.

1. Regular Confession

Regular confession keeps your soul in order. It is God's means of ridding you of and preserving you from the greatest evil in the world—sin. For this reason it is a source of peace and joy.

In the Sacrament of Penance (1) you receive *sanctifying grace* if it has been lost by mortal sin (this grace is increased if it had not been lost); (2)

your *sins are forgiven;* (3) you are freed from *eternal* punishment due to any mortal sin, and from a part, at least, of the *temporal punishment* due to your sins; (4) you receive *actual grace,* which is God's help to enable you to do good and avoid sin in the future; (5) you get back the *merits* of the good works you have lost by mortal sin.

Remember that the most important part of confession is not so much the telling of your sins, as *perfect sorrow* for them. Your contrition is perfect when you are sorry because your sins offended God, whom you should love above all things for His own sake. But contrition is also a hatred for the sins you committed, with a firm purpose of sinning no more. This means that you must really want to make up your mind not to sin any more and to try hard to keep away from whatever leads to sin, such as bad companions, bad places, bad reading. If you do not really want to keep away from mortal sin and from whatever will surely lead you into it, you make a bad confession.

In *confessing sins of impurity,* remember the following:

1. If you have real *mortal* sins to confess, then you must tell what you did and how often you did it. A confessor must know the kind of sin (self-abuse, immodest embracing, fornication) and the number of times; otherwise he may not give absolution. This does not mean that you must give a detailed description of your thoughts or acts.

2. If you are confessing sins of impurity and you mean only *venial* sins (negligence in regard to

thoughts, lack of sufficient reason in external acts) or mere *temptations* (imaginations or feelings that were not wilful), then indicate this to the confessor by saying, "I had bad thoughts, but they were not wilful" or "I tried to get rid of them." Otherwise he may think you mean mortal sins.

3. If you wish to confess *doubtful* sins (you doubt about consent, or whether you confessed the matter before), mention your doubt. Strictly speaking, doubtful sins do not have to be confessed, though it is better to do so, unless your confessor decides otherwise. Nor do you have to abstain from Holy Communion when you merely doubt whether you have sinned. You must be absolutely sure of having committed a mortal sin before you can say that you are not able to go to Communion. However, you should make an act of perfect contrition which will dispose your soul for the reception of the Sacrament.

4. If you have *difficulties* in regard to chastity or if you are inclined to be scrupulous, you should have a regular confessor. His advice will be more valuable since he will know the condition of your soul and the problems you must meet. Trust him, for God commissioned him to be your friend and your soul's guardian.

Go to Confession every week or at least once a month. This will enable you not only to cleanse your soul from sin, but also to correct your faults and keep yourself pleasing to God. It is one of the best means of keeping courtship clean and happy.

2. Frequent Holy Communion

Frequent Holy Communion, because of its wonderful effects, is the surest guarantee of keeping your youth and company-keeping pure and happy.

1. Holy Communion *unites you more closely with Jesus,* the Model of purity and the Author of all spiritual energy and holiness. You live in Him and He lives in you, for He said, "He who eats My Flesh and drinks My Blood, abides in Me and I in him."

2. Holy Communion gives you an increase of *sanctifying grace,* which makes you an adopted child of God, a temple of the Holy Ghost, and gives you a right to heaven. Sanctifying grace is the life of your soul, while mortal sin is its death. Our Lord said, "Unless you eat the Flesh of the Son of man and drink His Blood, you shall not have life in you." Sanctifying grace also makes you holy and pleasing to God. It adorns your soul with the only kind of beauty that is really worth striving for.

3. Holy Communion gives you sacramental or *actual grace,* which entitles you to special help in times of temptation and in the discharge of your duties, for it enlightens your mind and strengthens your will to do good and avoid evil. For this reason Holy Communion is a medicine for your soul when it becomes sick because of sin.

4. Holy Communion remits a part, or all, of the *temporal punishments* due to your sins.

5. Holy Communion is the best assurance that your *prayers will be heard,* if it is God's will; for

Jesus said, "If you abide in Me, and if My words abide in you, ask whatever you will and it shall be done to you." No prayer can be more effective than that said after Holy Communion when Jesus is present in your heart as God and Man, as your best Friend, ready to help you by means of the many graces He wishes to grant you. At Holy Communion you can ask Him to help you overcome the temptations you meet with in the world. He will give you the strength you need to keep pure and to be faithful to His holy commandments which are the foundation of true happiness. You should fear nothing, if you are equipped with the strongest spiritual weapon—Holy Communion. It prevents mortal sin—the greatest evil in the world—from taking root in your soul and even washes away the stains of venial sin so long as you have no affection for it nor desire to commit it in the future. The coming of Jesus in Holy Communion awakens new love in your heart and encourages you to live in purity and sinlessness, which is a necessary condition for happiness.

Our Lord wants you to receive Holy Communion often. It was for this reason that He gave you this Sacrament as a source of grace so that you might live as a good Catholic and save your soul. This was His last will expressed at the Last Supper: "Take and eat; this is My Body, which is being given for you; do this in remembrance of Me." As priests say Mass each day and receive Holy Communion to fulfill this last wish of Jesus, the faithful should do likewise by receiving Holy Communion daily if it is at all possible. For the first four centuries of Christianity the people received Holy Communion each time they assisted at Mass, for Communion is one of the principal parts of Mass. You miss so very much when you neglect to receive Communion during Mass. It is not a complete Mass. At the consecration you have given the heavenly Father His own beloved Son as the greatest gift you could offer Him in adoration, thanksgiving, atonement and petition; at Communion the heavenly Father wishes to return that Gift to you as the best He can offer you; but you refuse the Gift. And you need Jesus so very much; He does not need you! Live according to this principle: Always a Communion at my Mass.

Holy Mother Church earnestly wishes that you go to Holy Communion often, even daily, if possible. She speaks in the name of our Lord through the voice of Pope Pius X, the Pope of the Eucharist, "All the faithful, married or single, young or old, even children from the time of their first Communion are invited to go to Holy Communion frequently; yes, daily." Holy Mother Church requires only two things: (a) the state of grace. This means you must be free from every mortal sin and must have made up your mind never to commit a mortal sin again. Doubts about whether you are in the state of grace or not do not keep you from receiving. Make an act of contrition and go without any fear. You must be certain that you have committed a mortal sin before you can say that you may not receive. Venial sins do not keep you away. Be sorry for them and come to the Holy Table. The fact that you were not at Confession does not keep you away, as long as you are not in the state of mortal sin. Confession at least every two or three weeks is advisable for frequent communicants, but not necessary. If you cannot receive Holy Communion each morning, go at least on Sundays. (b) A right and good intention. This means that you should not go out of mere habit, or because others are going, or because you want to be seen by people. You should go to please God, to be united with Him by love, and to receive Holy Communion as a divine medicine for your sins and faults.

The saints, too, urge you by their words and example to receive Communion often. It was especially by receiving this heavenly food that they became saints.

Your own soul urges you to frequent Communion. It needs this spiritual food and strength to keep from sin and become holy. Your most important duty in life is to save your soul by serving God.

All that you desire in this life—peace and joy, success and health—depends upon God's blessing, which you receive above all when you are united with Jesus in Holy Communion. Come to Holy Communion daily if you can!

3. Prayer

Prayer is an unfailing means of grace and salvation. Our Lord said, "Ask and you shall receive." It is a particularly strong defense in time of temptation, for God will come to your aid when you call upon Him in your struggle against the serpent of impurity.

Try to be always on friendly terms with God by getting into the good habit of praying frequently during the day by means of little ejaculatory prayers and aspirations. If you regularly spend some time with God each day, you will find it easy to call upon Him when you need Him. Prayer lifts you above the sordid things of this world. It purifies your mind and strengthens your will. It keeps your soul seeking after God alone—the real purpose of life! With the weapon of prayer at your disposal, you are invincible.

Prayer will keep you very close to your best Friends—Jesus and Mary. Never let a day pass without asking Them to keep you from sin. Never go on a date without first asking Their blessing and protection and presence. A powerful prayer that has always kept young people pure and happy is the Holy Rosary. Pledge yourself to say it daily, especially if you are contemplating marriage. You can hardly make a better preparation. Keep your conversation with God, Our Lady, the angels, the saints; and you will walk among the stars!

4. Self-denial

A general spirit of self-denial is manifested by self-control. This is most important if you want to keep your dating chaste and happy. Self-control can be exercised in these ways:

1. Though you cannot prevent feeling pleasurable sensations and disturbing imaginations, and cannot

at times get rid of them, yet *your will can refrain from consenting to and approving them;* it can refrain from any external action that these things may urge you to do. Your will can avoid even the sources of stimulation so that the sexual passions not even aroused, e.g., questionable books and movies, improper speech and intimacies.

2. *Keep interested in something;* otherwise you may easily turn to amuse yourself with conduct that is either sinful in itself or that quickly leads to sin. This will keep you from developing a morbid interest in sex.

3. Cultivate a sincere, *wholesome attitude* that sees other things in life besides sex, so that you may not react readily to sexual suggestions.

4. Never let a day pass without *denying yourself some lawful pleasure* in eating, drinking, or entertainment for the love of God. If you can deny yourself in little things, you will be able to deny yourself in time of temptation.

Your cross in life is these temptations, these forbidden yet attractive pleasures. But Christ said, "If any man will come after Me, let him deny himself, and take up his cross daily and follow Me . . . he that shall save his life shall lose it; and he that shall lose his life, for My sake, shall save it." By the cross of Christian chastity you will most assuredly suffer, but you have nothing to lose but everything worthwhile to gain. Hold fast to the glory of your shining innocence! Nothing you can ever gain will compensate you for its loss. Your fidelity to your ideals may cost you much in money, in friends, in sacrifice.

But the surrender of your ideals will cost you more. For a passing gain you will barter eternity. A good conscience will be your sure reward. Only the heart without a stain knows perfect peace and joy.

5. Avoiding Occasions of Sin

Avoiding occasions of sin is but a form of self-denial. You need God's grace if you wish to be pure, but you must cooperate with that grace. You may receive the Sacraments frequently, attend novena services, make the First Fridays—all with the intention of not sinning against purity in your company-keeping. And yet you may not be using the means at your command to avoid the proximate occasions of sinning. If you know that someone or something is an immediate occasion of sin for you, avoid that person or thing. You cannot be pure if you insist on putting yourself in danger of losing your purity, by deliberately remaining in a parked car with your friend in some lonely place, or by remaining together for a long time indulging in "petting" and "necking," kissing and embracing. Your prayers to God for purity will be lies if you expect Him to save you from sin when you knowingly and willingly place yourself in the immediate occasions of sin. Until you have given up these occasions, your reception of the sacraments will continue to be hypocrisy. Do not sell your soul to the devil to win over or hold on to a young man or woman. You are losing everything but gaining nothing save misery and unhappiness, and possibly eternal damnation.

Safety lies in avoiding the danger. (If you play with fire you will burn yourself.) If you needlessly expose yourself to the danger of unchastity, you will rarely go unharmed. Therefore build a fence of self-denial around your virtue. Avoid all sources of temptation that can be sensibly shunned. Be extremely reserved in allowing even morally permissible favors to a lover. Learn to enjoy one another's company without physical contact. Follow the Legion of Decency list and refrain from going to motion pictures that are even partly objectionable. Do not read the "spotted" magazines and books unless there is some good reason for doing so. Above all, shun the company of questionable people, remembering the adage: "Tell me who you go with and I'll tell you who you are."

6. Love of Jesus and Mary

A deep love for Christ is a strong motive for chastity, and chastity is the most practical expression of your sincere love for Christ, for He said, "If you love Me, keep My commandments." This love is further proved by the frequent reception of the sacraments and by prayer and self-sacrifice. Remember that Jesus is your best friend and that He is always ready to help you keep your heart clean.

If you sincerely cultivate Mary's friendship also, you will be pure. To be her true child, you must love the things she loves and hate the things she hates. Purity is her favorite virtue. She hates nothing more than sin, for she has crushed the head of the infernal serpent. Call upon her especially in time of temptation. With her help you will triumph over the evil spirit who tempts you. She will give you the necessary help to achieve the ideal to which she inspires you. Never let a day pass without saying your Holy Rosary and three "Hail Marys" in honor of her Immaculate Conception for the grace of purity; follow these by the invocation, "O Mary, by thy Immaculate Conception make my body pure and my soul holy."

Pray for the grace and strength of the saints. They had a nature like yours. But "they had what it takes": the grace of God and their own Christian heroism. They would not dilly-dally with the occasion of sin. If you do not see eye to eye with the saints, you are the one out of focus. They knew and loved Jesus and Mary. They saw the value of their bodies and souls. They understood the language of heaven and hell.

You are called to the same Christian heroism. To remain pure is a big task; it calls for the best that is in you. Alone—without the grace of God—you cannot accomplish this task; with His grace, you are all-powerful. You obtain the grace of God especially through the sacraments, prayer and self-denial. Use these God-given aids conscientiously, and your youth will be clean and happy.

CHAPTER VI

CHOOSING A PARTNER

Care and Common Sense

The decision of supreme importance in your life is the choice of a helpmate for life. The consequences of that choice reach even into eternity. It follows that your choice should be made with the greatest care, prudence and wisdom. Company-keeping and courtship have no other reason for existence except to assist you in becoming better acquainted and in making a wise choice. Acquaintance and friendship between the sexes should be fairly extensive. Dances, dramatics, and social affairs are designed to promote such acquaintance. Meet many young people of good reputation and character. Mingle and talk with them in a friendly way. Learn their interests, disposition and character. Out of many friendships you are likely to form one based upon disposition, character, training, outlook and convictions—one which will ripen into conjugal love.

In courtship you must first of all *be true to yourself*. Because a choice is made while the emotions tend to disturb the even functioning of the mind, you stand at that time in particular need of guidance. The advice of parents, the priest, and of other sensible people of experience should be sought. Do not make the mistake of confiding in no one about your choice of a helpmate in life. This would close the door to many helpful suggestions and perhaps open it to an unfortunate marriage. Love is blind.

Common sense can give it eyes. So keep at least one ear attuned to the voice of reason. Do not be content to gaze upon the beauty of the face of your sweetheart, but learn to penetrate to the disposition and character with which you must live when the bloom of youth has gone. Beauty vanishes, but character remains. Do not rely on superficial factors. Character, piety, disposition, intelligence, understanding, sympathy and unselfishness are the things which count in creating a happy home and a permanent union. Be on your guard against elements which make for separation and divorce. One of the chief causes of these disorders is that the couple discovers after marriage that they are mismated; they have little in common. They are uncongenial in temperament and disposition; they differ in moral character and in religious outlook, in culture and tastes. Association loses its charm; boredom sets in and finally leads to aversion.

Test yourself to find out if you are really called to married life with this particular person. As soon as you realize that such a union does not and cannot appeal to you, gently discontinue the courtship regardless of consequences. It is better to part as friends in good time than to be compelled either to live together very unhappily for life, or to separate as enemies later on. After all, it is the purpose of courtship to learn this very thing.

Courtship should be entered upon with a deep sense of responsibility and mutual respect. Intelligent choice of a mate must not look only to mutual physical attraction, but more so to harmony of

tastes, feelings, desires, aspirations, and of temperament. It must weigh spiritual more than physical
values. What has begun as a mere sex intimacy
is not likely to end in a happy marriage.

In courtship you must also *be honest and honorable towards your partner*. Reveal yourself and your
family and personal stature with sincerity and truth
to the extent to which he or she has the right to
this information. However, there are certain things
of a family or personal nature one need not and must
not tell, such as personal repented sin. They are
best left buried and forgotten. No one except God
should ever know of past sins. As soon as you know
that a person has no prospect whatever of marrying
you, you are in duty bound to discontinue receiving
his attentions. After you are engaged to be married,
you can no longer keep company honorably with
others, as long as this engagement holds.

Listen to the wise voice of the ancient Church
which has seen millions of young couples through
happy marriages and has only their earthly success
and eternal happiness at heart. The Catholic Church
warns you in advance that you will pay a heavy pen-
alty for negligence, haste, and rashness in choosing
a partner. Before she admits candidates to the
priesthood, she requires them to spend long years
in training and discipline, meditating all the while
on the seriousness of the step they contemplate. Yet
Holy Orders imposes no obligation of greater duration than that imposed by matrimony. Refrain from
beginning to keep regular company too soon. If you
begin to do so at sixteen or seventeen years, you

expose yourself either to the danger of a premature marriage with its frequent mistake of poor choice or you court the hardly lesser evil of an immoderately long courtship with the attendant disadvantages. You tie yourself down to one person and thus lose the social advantages and contacts that will have a great influence upon your later life. You expose yourself in a special way to temptations against chastity, because this love affair may be a very prolonged one, and the danger of violating chastity increases as the affection is prolonged. If you begin "to go steady" while you are a student, you will find it almost impossible to do justice to your studies.

Since courtship limits your interest to a single person, it should not be undertaken until you are in a position seriously to consider marriage in the not too distant future. This presupposes that you have attained the age to understand the great responsibilities of marriage and that you have enough financial resources to establish and maintain a home. Marrying in haste nearly always means repenting bitterly at leisure. Do not prefer to be sorry to being certain.

While the Church warns against courtships of undue brevity, *she likewise counsels against those of excessive length.* No hard and fast rule can be laid down determining the exact length of courtship. It should be of sufficient duration to allow young people to learn the character and disposition of each other quite well. This can usually be done in a period ranging from six months to a year. Ordinarily regular company-keeping should not be protracted much beyond a year. Aside from the obvious moral dangers involved, long courtships are undesirable because they often end in no marriage or in an unhappy marriage. Grievous injustice can be done to the girl if the man terminates the courtship after monopolizing her attention for several years, and depriving her of other opportunities. Courtship is not the end but the vestibule leading to the great Sacrament.

How to Choose a Marriage Partner

The following questions will not only help you to fit yourself for leading a worthy and holy married life, but also enable you to choose a partner in marriage intelligently. These qualifications apply to men and women alike.

I. Friendship

1. Is your friendship morally beneficial? Are you morally better or worse for having been with him, and what can you expect in the future? Would marriage with him help you to observe God's commandments and practice your religious duties faithfully?

2. Imagine a crisis in your life (poverty, sickness) that might demand a high quality of virtue to remain faithful to God. Would he be a help to the practice of such virtue?

3. Does he drink too much? Gamble?

4. Does he want to indulge in petting, passionate kissing, even at the expense of chastity?

5. Does he control his temper? Has he a sense of humor? Can he keep a secret?

6. Does he practice his religion?

7. What are his views on divorce, on having children, on Catholic education, on frequenting the sacraments?

8. Can you actually point out any definite virtuous qualities, or are they put on for your benefit now?

II. Agreement

1. Is there at least a reasonable degree of similarity between you in regard to the recreations you like?

2. Could you both enjoy staying at home in the evening, especially when children come?

3. Are there any habits now that not only get on your nerves but which you find extraordinarily difficult to overlook?

4. Do you both fit into about the same kind of social life?

5. Does he get along with your family and you with his?

6. Have you both sufficient health for marriage?

7. What are his habits of life: cleanliness, orderliness, good manners, good grammar?

8. Are you able to harmonize judgments on things that pertain to family life: food, kind of house, furnishings, etc.?

9. Have you the same religion and the same standards concerning its practice?

10. Have you the same attitude towards children and their education?

11. Do you feel at ease together, regardless of

what you talk about? If you do not meet for some time, are you able to take up where you left off, with something of the naturalness of a family reunion, or do you have to try to work up an acquaintance all over again?

12. Has he a nagging or reforming disposition?

13. Do you see his failings, and are you willing to tolerate them? Does he admit them and is he willing to get over them?

14. With children in mind, would you say that this person would be just the right other parent for them?

III. Self-Sacrifice

1. Is your prospective companion thoughtful of others and has he the power of self-discipline?

2. In his home does he show thoughtfulness of parents and brothers and sisters, and do you get the impression that this is his regular attitude?

3. What little kindnesses, not only to you but to others, have you noticed in him?

4. When he is wrong, does he admit it and try to make up for it?

5. Does he easily and graciously pass over others' mistakes?

6. Does he look for sympathy too much?

7. Can he give sympathy willingly, or does some one else's trouble always bring out a greater trouble of his?

8. Does he show that he knows his temper, and that jealousy and other unpleasant traits ought to be controlled?

If it is a Wife You Want:

1. Can she cook and make the house a home?

2. Has she that womanly quality that instinctively puts things in order?

3. Would this girl be a real mother?

4. Could she bear children and sacrifice for them?

5. Could she give the child that early introduction to God that he would never forget?

6. Is she convinced that motherhood is an all-day and an all-night job?

7. How does she speak of children? How does she treat them?

8. What do her younger brothers and sisters think of her?

If it is a Husband You Want:

1. How does he like children?

2. Does he like to work? Can he hold a job?

3. Has he a sense of responsibility?

4. Is he "grown up," or does he have to be pampered?

5. Is he unduly jealous? A braggart? An alibi-artist? Is he courteous?

Such questions will bring you down to earth and keep you from estimating things merely on the score of fascination. Many of the po ıts are not in themselves important; the general pic ure that is created by the various answers is very important. Many points cannot be tested out before marriage, but glaring risks can be easily recognized. Though these characteristics need not be preset in a high degree at the time of marriage, the beginnings should be present, or at least a genuine willingness and effort to improve.

If there is question of reforming your friend, it should be done before, not after marriage. Do not put your faith in vague promises which seldom materialize. If you cannot get along agreeably before marriage, it is almost certain that you will not get along after marriage.

As soon as you have finally resolved to accept one another as mates, if no insurmountable hindrance is in the way, consult your pastor and set the date for your marriage. You should derive a certain satisfaction from the publication of the banns of marriage because you have nothing to be ashamed of.

Before marriage pay close attention to the instruction on marriage and its ethics given you by the priest. Read a popular and practical treatise on the subject. It may be advisable to make a general confession before entering the holy state of marriage. Penance is a second baptism. It will gratify you to know that you are beginning married life with a soul entirely free from every stain of sin. This is absolutely necessary for those who have sinned in courtship and have been receiving the Sacraments unworthily in consequence, lest they receive matrimony sacrilegiously and thus be bereft of its graces. Arrange for a devotional and inspiring church wedding with Holy Mass and the special blessing of God and of the Church. It will always be a beautiful and heartening memory for life.

Mixed Marriages

The nature and purpose of marriage demand true piety and virtue in both parties in order that they may assist and sanctify each other. There can be no true unity of mind and heart if they differ in this most essential matter of religious belief. The Church law says: "The Church most strictly forbids mixed marriages everywhere." (Canon 1060.) Thus she implicitly forbids courtship between Catholics and non-Catholics. When the Church does permit mixed marriages by granting special dispensation, it is only with reluctance and under certain well-defined conditions. The divine law forbidding these marriages when there is proximate danger to the faith of the Catholic party or their children cannot be dispensed by any human authority whatsoever.

Experience has proved the following facts about mixed marriages:

1. One of the great barriers to unity of mind and heart is difference in religion.

2. Mixed marriages have been and continue to be the cause of an alarming and ever-increasing number of fallen-away Catholics.

3. The majority of the children of mixed marriages are either not reared in the faith or early lose their faith.

4. The modern non-Catholic's attitude toward marriage is so different from the Catholic's attitude that mixed marriage almost invariably leads to serious disagreement between the man and the woman, particularly about birth control, Catholic education, religious practices.

5. A non-Catholic can always end marriage in divorce, which is in complete opposition to Christ's law. But marrriage for the Catholic is a lifelong contract. Christ so ordained it, and the Catholic so regards it.

6. If the Catholic in a mixed marriage is faithful to his religion, he is extremely lonely; he feels isolated from his partner, and he finds it almost impossible to explain the situation to the children.

7. Marriage itself presents enough problems without adding the problems that are created by religious differences.

Since the possible marriage with a non-Catholic, grand, noble and honorable though he or she be, presents so many strong dangers to the faith of the Catholic concerned, you must be careful to tell your confessor at once of the hazardous courtship. This should be done in order to obtain advice.

If you insist on marrying a non-Catholic, you should take the person to the priest, at least six weeks before the marriage that there may be ample time for the necessary instructions. Though the non-Catholic does not intend to become a Catholic, he must at least know what his future partner believes, what promises must be made, the nature of marriage, its duties, responsibilities, and privileges.

Catholics should marry their own kind. Conversions before marriage are often more or less pretended and are seldom the fruit of sincere conviction. Those who embrace the Catholic religion merely to obtain a certain partner in matrimony usually are no credit to it. There are exceptions, but experience shows that very few mixed marriages develop fortunately for both parties. Nine out of every ten Catholics who contract a mixed marriage do it to their own and their children's serious detriment. If you are prudent and eager for peace and happiness, you will resolutely prefer the single life to any kind of mixed marriage.

A Trinity of Love

Love, courtship and marriage are part of a divine plan. The flame of love that burns in the bosom of sweethearts is kindled by no human hands, but by a spark from the love that is eternal and divine. It is God's perfect gift to man.

If you have always loved, prized and guarded purity and innocence as your most precious personal possession, your wedding day will be a truly happy day. If you have prepared for marriage by a courtship characterized from beginning to end by a high mutual esteem, ideal love and devotion, angelic purity and unfailing self-restraint, begotten by the fear as well as the love of the Lord and a tender, reverential regard for one another, then you will taste the sweetest happiness that God grants to man in this vale of tears when the priest binds you in the deathless union of the Sacrament of Matrimony. Then God will bless your union with that most wonderful of all His gifts, a little angel in human flesh. You will understand the fair romance and the sweet mystery of life when that baby binds your hearts still more closely together in a blessed trinity of love. You are not only husband and wife, but mother and father. You will love each other with a love as strong as life itself.

In that sanctuary of the home, a tabernacle of holy love, you come as near to that celestial paradise as you ever can on earth.

VARIOUS PRAYERS

A PRAYER FOR MY VOCATION

O my God, Thou who art the God of wisdom and counsel, Thou who readest in my heart the sincere will to please Thee alone and to govern myself with regard to my choice of a state of life entirely in conformity with Thy most holy desire; grant me by the intercession of the most Blessed Virgin, my Mother, and of my holy patrons, especially of St. Joseph and St. Aloysius, the grace to know what state of life I ought to choose, and when to embrace it, so that in it I may be able to pursue and increase Thy glory, and work out my salvation, and merit that heavenly reward which Thou hast promised to those that do Thy will. Amen. (Indulgence of 300 days, once a day. Pius X, May 6, 1905.)

A PRAYER TO THE HOLY SPIRIT

(Veni Sancte Spiritus)

Holy Spirit, come and shine
On my soul with beams divine,
Issuing from Thy radiance bright.
Come, O Father of the poor,
Ever bounteous of Thy store,
Come, my heart's unfailing Light!

Come, Consoler, kindest, best,
Come, my bosom's dearest Guest,
Sweet refreshment, sweet respose.

Rest in labor, coolness sweet,
Tempering the burning heat,
Truest comfort of my woes.

O divinest Light, impart
Unto my poor yearning heart
Plenteous streams from love's bright flood.
But for Thy blest Deity,
Nothing pure in me could be;
Nothing harmless, nothing good.

Wash away each sinful stain;
Gently shed Thy gracious rain
On my dry and fruitless soul.
Heal each wound and bend my will,
Warm my heart benumbed and chill,
All my wayward steps control.

Unto me Thy faithful child,
Who in Thee confide in trial,
Deign Thy seven-fold gifts to send.
Grant me virtue's blest increase,
Grant a death of hope and peace,
Grant the joys that never end. Amen.

A PRAYER FOR A GOOD HUSBAND OR WIFE

O Jesus, Lover of the young, the dearest Friend I
have, in all confidence I open my heart to You to beg
Your light and assistance in the important task of
planning my future. Give me the light of Your
grace, that I may decide wisely concerning the person who is to be my partner through life. Dearest
Jesus, send me such a one whom in Your divine
wisdom You judge best suited to be united with me
in marriage. May his (her) character reflect some
of the traits of Your own Sacred Heart. May he

(she) be upright, loyal, pure, sincere and noble, so that with united efforts and with pure and unselfish love we both may strive to perfect ourselves in soul and body, as well as the children it may please You to entrust to our care. Bless our friendship before marriage, that sin may have no part in it. May our mutual love bind us so closely, that our future home may ever be most like Your own at Nazareth.

O Mary Immaculate, sweet Mother of the young, to your special care I entrust the decision I am to make as to my future husband (wife). You are my guiding Star! Direct me to the person with whom I can best co-operate in doing God's Holy Will, with whom I can live in peace, love and harmony in this life, and attain to eternal joys in the next. Amen.

PRAYERS FOR PURITY

Jesus Lover of chastity, Mary, Mother most pure, and Joseph, chaste guardian of the Virgin, to you I come at this hour, begging you to plead with God for me. I earnestly wish to be pure in thought, word, and deed in imitation of your own holy purity.

Obtain for me, then, a deep sense of modesty which will be reflected in my external conduct. Protect my eyes, the windows of my soul, from anything that might dim the luster of a heart that must mirror only Christlike purity.

And when the "Bread of angels becomes the Bread of men" in my heart at Holy Communion, seal it forever against the suggestions of sinful pleasures.

Heart of Jesus, Fount of all purity, have mercy on us.

Let my heart, O Lord, be made immaculate, that I may not be ashamed. (300 days.)

Grant, we beseech Thee, Almighty and everlasting God, that we may attain to purity of mind and body through the inviolate virginity of the most pure Virgin Mary. Amen. (500 days.)

O Virgin Mother, who was never defiled by the stain of sin, neither actual nor original, to thee I commend and entrust the purity of my heart. (300 days.)

Hail Mary, etc. O Mary, by thy Immaculate Conception make my body pure and my soul holy. (300 days—repeat three times.)

Make my heart and my body clean, Holy Mary. (300 days.)

O my Queen, O my Mother, remember that I am thine own. Keep me, guard me as thy property and possession.

Saint Joseph, father and guardian of virgins, into whose faithful keeping were entrusted innocence itself, Christ Jesus, and Mary, the Virgin of virgins, I pray and beseech thee through Jesus and Mary, those pledges so dear to thee, to keep me from all uncleanness, and to grant that my mind may be untainted, my heart pure and by body chaste; help me always to serve Jesus and Mary in perfect chastity. Amen. (3 years.)

TAN·BOOKS

TAN Books was founded in 1967 to preserve the spiritual, intellectual and liturgical traditions of the Catholic Church. At a critical moment in history TAN kept alive the great classics of the Faith and drew many to the Church. In 2008 TAN was acquired by Saint Benedict Press. Today TAN continues its mission to a new generation of readers.

From its earliest days TAN has published a range of booklets that teach and defend the Faith. Through partnerships with organizations, apostolates, and mission-minded individuals, well over 10 million TAN booklets have been distributed.

More recently, TAN has expanded its publishing with the launch of Catholic calendars and daily planners—as well as Bibles, fiction, and multimedia products through its sister imprints Catholic Courses (CatholicCourses.com) and Saint Benedict Press (SaintBenedictPress.com).

Today TAN publishes over 500 titles in the areas of theology, prayer, devotions, doctrine, Church history, and the lives of the saints. TAN books are published in multiple languages and found throughout the world in schools, parishes, bookstores and homes.

For a free catalog, visit us online at
TANBooks.com

Or call us toll-free at
(800) 437-5876